A STUDY OF THOMAS HARDY

A STUDY OF
THOMAS HARDY

BY

ARTHUR SYMONS

Author of

Studies in Two Literatures; The Symbolist Movement in
Literature; Studies in Prose and Verse; William Blake

WITH A PORTRAIT

BY

ALVIN COBURN

HASKELL HOUSE PUBLISHERS LTD.
Publishers of Scarce Scholarly Books
NEW YORK. N. Y. 10012
1971

First Published 1927

HASKELL HOUSE PUBLISHERS LTD.
Publishers of Scarce Scholarly Books
280 LAFAYETTE STREET
NEW YORK, N. Y. 10012'

Library of Congress Catalog Card Number: 77-160427

Standard Book Number 8383-1297-7

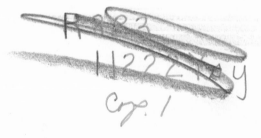

Printed in the United States of America

THOMAS HARDY has a kind of naked face, in which you see the brain always working, with an almost painful simplicity—just saved from being painful by a humorous sense of external things, which becomes a kind of intellectual criticism. When I saw him on the 2nd of June 1926, in his own house—it was his birthday and he eighty-six—it was evident to me that the burden of those years meant very little to him. There was the same small wiry man, whose genius was evident in his aspect: and there was the same kind of pained perplexity in his face which I have always noticed; and there was the same grim sardonic humour and the same vitality.

In all his work Hardy is concerned with one thing, seen under two aspects : not civilization, nor manners, but the principle of life itself, invisibly realized as Sex, seen visibly in the world as what we call Nature. He is a fatalist, rather a determinist, and he studies the workings of fate, or law (ruling through inexorable moods, or humours), in the main vivifying and disturbing influence in life, Woman. In his earlier books he is somewhat careful over the reputation of the heroines, gradually he allows them more liberty, with a franker treatment of instinct and its consequences. It is rather difficult to get accustomed to Hardy, or to do him justice without doing him more than justice. He is invariably right, always a seer, when he writing about " the seasons in their moods, morning and evening, night and dawn, winds in their different

tempers, freer waters, and mists, shades
and silences, and the voices of inanimate
things." What gravity and intimacy in
his numbering of them! He is always
right, always faultless in matter and style,
when he is showing that " the impression-
able peasant leads a fuller, more dramatic
life than the pachydermatous King." But
he requires a certain amount of emotion
to shake off the lethargy natural to his
style, and when he has merely a dull fact
to mention, he says it like this: " He
reclined on his couch in the sitting-room
and extinguished the light." In the next
sentence, when he is interested in express-
ing the impalpable emotion of the situation, we get this faultless and uncommon
use of words. " The night came in, and
took up its place there, unconcerned and
indifferent; the night which had already
swallowed up his happiness, and was now

7

digesting it listlessly; and was ready to swallow up the happiness of a thousand other people with as little disturbance of mien."

The fact is, that there is a lethargy natural to his style, and that is one reason of the frequent tediousness of his prose. Take this sentence which is as vivid as a vision : a vision I myself have often seen in Auverne, as for instance when I went up from Clermont-Ferrand to the height of the Puy-de Dôme in a *diligence,* which was by no means comfortable. " Looking at the van from the back, the spectator could see there, through its interior, a square piece of the same sky and land-scape that he saw without, but intruded on by the profiles of the seated passengers who, as they rumbled onwards, their lips moving and heads nodding in animated private converse, remained in cheerful unconsciousness that their mannerisms and facial peculiarities were sharply defined to the public eye." Take this one for contrast. "Women's prescriptive inferiority had stalked into the sunlight, which had invested it with the freshness of an originality."

In Hardy's feeling for Nature—which is primitive and not essentially animal—curiosity seems at times to broaden into an intimate kind of emotion. The knowledge of women confirms him in a wise suspension of judgment; his knowledge of Nature brings him nearer to the consoling and unchanging element in the world. The heath, the village with its peasantry (he said to me in June, 1926, "Alas, the peasants have almost died out!"), the change of every hour among the fields and on the roads, mean more to him, in a sense, than even the spectacle of men and women in their blind and painful and absorbing struggle for existence. All the quiet, happy entertainment which he gets out of life comes to him from his interpretation of the peasant, as himself a rooted part of the earth, translating the dumbness of the fields into humour. The peasants have been compared with Shakespeare's; that is because he has the Shakespearean sense of their placid vegetable existence by the side of hurrying animal life, to which they act the part of chorus, with an unconscious wisdom in their close, narrow and undistracted view of things.

In regard to that subtle and strong and extraordinary novel *A Pair of Blue Eyes* (1873) Mr. Brenneck—in reference to the devastation caused by the antics of Chance or of Destiny, symbolised by Nemesis—notices the trend of Hardy's conception.

"As the dainty Elfride may be said to represent, in herself, the volatility and capriciousness of Chance—herself subject to Casualty in the form of tragic coincidences and to Fate to the form of heredity—so the dark-robed, ominous figure of Mrs. Jethway, casting sinister shadows over even the brightest moments of the story, may be said to be an incarnation of the spirit of the Three Sisters or of the cankering fury of the ancient Nemesis." Lionel Johnson points out certain extravagances that occur in this novel : "Elfride, Stephen and Knight, that tragic trio in various combinations, repeating the same scenes, meeting under conditions of curious strangeness; until they meet at last, Elfride in her coffin, the wife of neither; and the rival lovers, with their strained old intimacy of master and pupil, travelling in the train that carries her; each having concealed from the other his purpose of going down to find her, both ignorant of her death."

This final, unforgiveable tragedy comes about by a triple misunderstanding; and Elfride remains the victim of this evil lack of comprehension on the part of her two lovers. She is always dainty, emotional, pure, lovely, inexperienced, wilful, capricious, somewhat passionate, given over to her shifting impressions, uncertain of herself, whose few casual slips are not owing to any inner hotness of her blood. She has unwittingly let her first lover die; she conceives a curious liking for Stephen Smith, from which ensues the usual elopement and her return to her home and his departure. She conceives an actual passion for Henry Knight the writer, whom she is on the point of marrying. In the midst of this occurs the most amazing accident I have read in any novel, in which Knight having lost his footing on the edge of a cliff hangs for an interminable length of time, only supported from certain death by propping his feet on a piece of granite, which is some slight distance below the edge of this sheer precipice. How one's breath is held in suspense during nineteen pages which express more agony that even those pages in *Lavengro* which describe a paroxysm of fear which has never been surpassed in sheer nervous horror. In these pages of Hardy the suspense is drawn out so minutely and with such immense continuity of perfected art, that one imagines the man's horrible situation, during which "Time closed up like a fan before him. He reclined hand in hand with the world in its infancy. Not a blade, not an insect, which spoke of the present, was between

him and the past. He saw himself at one
extremity of the fan, face to face with the
beginning and all the intermediate centuries simultaneously. The world was to
some extent turned upside down for him.
Rain descended from below. Beneath his
feet was aerial space and the Unknown."
It is Elfride who saves him by a woman's
magnificent instinct. She simply un-
dresses under the pouring rain, having
absolutely nothing between her and the
weather but her exterior robe: all the rest
of her clothing she had woven into a rope,
which she flung down to him, up which he
climbed, finding himself saved at last;
and, moved by an irresistable impulse,
they rushed into one another's arms.

What ruins Elfride's chances with
Knight is that horrible suspicion of her
past which creeps over him. She tells
him the truth, almost the entire truth:

but her love for him is so absolute that
she hesitates in her confessions : to such
a point that he says to her : " You must
forget me. We shall not marry." How
much anguish passed into her soul at those
words from him was told by the look of
supreme torture she wore. She makes a
last attempt to recapture him by appear-
ing in his rooms, alone. The scene is
interrupted by the arrival of her father in
a state of intense fury,who takes her away
with him. " Knight's eyes followed her,
the last moment begetting in him a frantic
hope that she would turn her head. She
passed on, and never looked back." She
leaves him to a dreadful conflict; he
knowing all the time that she loved him,
that he could not leave off loving her, and
that he could not marry her. The man
was evidently wrong-headed : he was as
utterly incapable of passion as of forgiv-

ing her. And one asks : what was there to forgive? And I would answer : Less than nothing. And this is Hardy's comment. " Perhaps it was human and certainly natural that Knight never once thought whether he did not owe her a little sacrifice for her unchary devotion in saving his life."

As Flaubert invented the rhythm of every sentence I choose this sentence from *Madame Bovary.* " Et Emma se mit à rire, d'un rire atroce, frénétique, déséspéré, croyant voir la face hideuse du misérable, qui se dressait dans les ténèbres éternelles comme un épouvantement." Aeschylus might have made Clytemnestra utter such words as these on her lying lips in her atrocious speech after she had slain Agamemnon. With this compare a sentence of Petrus Borel. " I have often heard that certain insects were made for the amusement of children; perhaps man also was made for the same pleasure of superior beings, who delight in torturing him, and disport themselves in his pains." This is a sentence which might almost have been written by Hardy, so exactly does it state, in an image like one of his own, the satiric centre of his philosophy. Take, for instance, these solemn and tragic sentences in *The Return of the Native.* "Yet, upon the whole, neither the man nor the woman lost dignity by sudden death. Misfortune had struck them gracefully, cutting off their erratic histories with a catastrophic dash."

A Laodicean, that strange and subtle novel, woven together with the learned casuistry of a Jesuit, has much of Hardy himself in it : George Somerset, the architect, is I imagine a kind of self-portrait. It is written in a dispassionate manner, with an undercurrent of irony, and what is astonishing is the clash and contest over the mere fact of rebuilding the ancient castle of the De Stancys, of all these characters, including the rivalry of Somerset and Havill, the intervention of Dare, the dissolute and degraded son of Captain de Stancy, on behalf of his father whom he wants to marry Paula Powers, for her beauty and her immense wealth and her other possessions, in order to profit from this transaction, which fails; and this defeated criminal takes a mean revenge in the end by setting fire to the Castle which just then, having been restored, is empty. Dare, is of course, meant for a modern type of an ineffectual Iago. No sooner have Paula and Somerset been married—they were staying at that time at the Lord Quantock hotel—than they hear that the Castle is on fire. They

have just made some plans which are frus-
trated by this catastrophe. They watch
with horror the demolition of all but its
most ancient part; and, on their return
to the hotel, decide on building a new
house near the ruins. Somerset says to
Paula : " You, Paula, will be yourself
again, and recover, if you have not already, from the warp given to your mind
by the mediævalism of the Castle." She
concludes with a suppressed sigh that the
new house will show the modern spirit
for evermore. " But, George, I wish my
Castle wasn't burnt and I wish you were
a de Stancy! " Such is the cynical but
satisfying end of this intricate study,
which reminds me to a certain extent of
Stendhal.

Paula is ambiguous, and, fond of
Somerset as she is, it is only near the end
of the novel that she confesses her love to

him (now that the murder is out) and as desperately as any woman can care for any man. We get a wonderful glimpse of her. " Her imperception of his feeling was the very sublimity of maiden inno- cence if it were real; if not, well, her coquetry was no great sin." Somerset makes love to her under a thunderstorm.

" Will you love me, Paula? "

" You may love me."

" And don't you love me in return? "

" I love you to love me."

After the return of her uncle Abner Powers, who has the face of a smelter and the manner of a Dutchman, takes her abroad with him to the Riviera, where Somerset finally arrives, at Monte Carlo, where he enters the Casino. " Here he was confronted by a heated phantasmagoria of tainted splendour and a high pressure of suspense that seemed to make the

air quiver." Gambling is one testimony
among many of the powerlessness of logic
when confronted with imagination. Dare
the traitor sends Paula a wire in the name
of Somerset asking her as he has lost a
hundred pounds to send him that amount,
and that he will be waiting on the Pont
Neuf at Genoa. De Stancy goes with
Paula's gold in a bag and finds Dare waiting for him on the bridge, to whom he
does not give the money. Paula, when
she hears of it, is offended. Abner goes
back to the church near the Castle where
he finds Dare; they have a sinister conver-
sation in the vestry, where Dare points out
to Abner that he knows as much of his
infamous career as Abner knows of his.
The result is two pistols levelled at one
another: but the ghoul refrains from
killing the criminal. When at Caen, de
Stancy tells her that the criminal is his

son, she turns her back on him and says—
there had been some mention of their
marriage : " You need not come again."
The two wandering lovers at last meet at
Etretat. She goes alone—like Porphyria
—to the room where Somerset lies on a
couch, crouches beside him and re-
proaches herself and him with roguish
solicitude. Paula has always been an
enigma : George has often been provok-
ing. And so they are married. She has a
nameless dread of returning to the Castle,
a fear that some uncanny influence of the
dead de Stancys would drive her again
from Somerset. She was unaware that
two criminals were mixed up in certain
base actions which led of dire necessity
to the conflagration : the ghoul Abner and
the culprit Dare.

It has often occurred to me to look at
the first and last sentence of a novel : it is
inconceivable how much depends on this
kind of curiosity. *Le Père Goriot* begins :
" Madame Vauquer, née de Conflans, est
une vieille femme qui, depuis quarante
ans, tient à Paris une pension bourgeoise
établie rue Neuve-Sainte-Généviève,
entre le Quartier Latin et le faubourg
Saint-Marceau." The end is immensely
cynical. " Les yeux de Rastignac
s'attachèrent presque avidement entre la
colonne de la place Vendôme et le Dôme
des Invalides, là où vivait ce beau monde
dans lequel il avait voulu pénétrer ! Il
lança sur cette ruche bourdonnante un
regard qui semblait par avance en pomper

le miel, et dit ce mot suprême :—A nous deux maintenant! Puis il revint à pied rue d'Arras, et alla dîner chez Madame de Nucingen." So as to show the sudden flashes of the genius of Balzac, I shall give three sentences: "Qui n'a pas pratiqué la rive gauche de la Seine, entre la rue Saint Jacques et la rue des Saints-Pères, ne connaît rien à la vie humaine! " " ' Eh! si les femmes de Paris savaient! ' se disait Rastignac." This sentence is worthy of Machiavelli. " Savez-vous comment on fait son chemin ici? par l'éclat du génie ou par l'adresse de la Corruption." Now turn to *Salammbô*: "C'était à Mégara, faubourg de Carthage, dans les jardins d'Hamilcar." Is there anything ominous in this sentence? No. " Salammbô retomba, la tête en arrière, par-dessus le dossier du trône,—blême, raidie, les lèvres ouvertes,—et ses cheveux dénoués pendaient jusqu' à terre. Ainsi mourut la fille d'Hamilcar pour avoir touché au manteau de Tanit." One must remember that Mâtho in the beginning offers her wine. At the end she had risen, a bowl of wine in her hand, which she was supposed to drink before she hands the bowl to Narr-Havas who is to become her husband. The wine she drank was the wine which engenders Death: the love-potion: and that was the revenge of Tanit.

This is my translation of the first and last sentence of *Boule de Suif*. "For several days, straggling remnants of the routed enemy had passed through the town." "And Boule de Suif wept on, and at times a sob which she could not repress broke out between two couplets in the darkness." Maupassant was the man of his period, and his period was that of Naturalism. In *Les Soirées de Medan,* the volume in which *Boule de Suif* appears, there is another story called *Sac au Dos,* in which another novelist made his appearance among the five who publicly affirmed their literary tendencies about the central figure of Zola. J. K. Huysmans, then at the outset of his slow and painful course through schools and experiments, was in time to sum up the tendencies of a new period, as significantly as Maupassant summed up in his short and brilliant and almost undeviating career the tendencies of that period in which Taine and science seemed to have at last found out the physical basis of life. Now it is a new realism which appeals to us : it is the turn of the soul. The battle which the *Soirées de Médan* helped to win has been won; having gained our right to deal with humble and unpleasant and sordidly tragic things in fiction, we are free to concern ourselves with other things. But though the period has passed and will not return, the masterpieces of the period remain. Among the masterpieces, not the least among them, is *Boule de Suif*.

Now turn to *Under the Greenwood Tree*. " To the dwellers in a wood, almost every species of tree has its voice as well as its features. And winter, which modifies the note of such trees as shed their leaves, does not destroy its individuality." This is the end, which comes after the marriage of Dick and Fancy, when they hear the sudden note of a bird. " ' O, 'tis the nightingale,' murmured she, and thought of a secret she should never tell." That is one of Hardy's unerring touches. Turn by comparison to *Two on a Tower,* a romance which was " the outcome of a wish to set the emotional history of two infinitesimal lives against the stupendous background of the stellar universe, and to impart to readers the sentiment that of these contesting magnitudes the smaller might be the greater to them as men. The first sentence is curious: "On an early winter morning, keen but not cold, when the vegetable world was a weird multitude of skeletons through whose ribs the sun shone freely, a gleaming landau came to a pause on the crest of a hill in Wessex." Here are two sinister touches: "weird" and "skeletons." The end in its sheer tragedy is utterly unexpected: for all of a sudden Viviette's lover who had deserted her for years appears, Swithin, who, bounding out on the roof of the tower, clasps her in his arms and kisses her passionately, saying: "Viviette, Viviette, I have come to marry you!" She utters a shriek of amazed joy

—such as was never heard on that tower before or since—and falls in his arms, clasping his neck. " Sudden joy after despair had touched an overstrained heart too smartly. Viviette was dead. The Bishop was avenged." This is a climax, but the book is not one of Hardy's greatest novels; there breathes across these pages a malevolent Spirit who disturbs the antics of those living puppets he cannot dislocate. And there are too many incongruities, degradations and malicious disgraces, which are beyond the domain of the Humanist; and these bodies seem to be seriously lacking in what one names the Soul.

There is no doubt that Hardy has dived deep into the works of French novelists and into the immortal pages of Rabelais, Voltaire, Swift and Petronius : in whose shameless Immorality, in whose evident

Bestiality, in whose open Lasciviousness, there is nothing that can offend the purest taste—that is to say of those whose taste is pure, and to whom what seems to the majority to be impure is essentially pure. *Jude the Obscure* is one of the most sexual novels I have ever read : it is immoral in the sense that sex itself is immoral; and it is perhaps the most unbiassed consideration of the more complicated questions of Sex which we can find in English fiction. And these dates are of interest. The scheme was jotted down in 1890 from notes made in 1867 and onwards; the scenes were revised in October 1892; the narrative was written in outline in 1892 and the spring of 1893, and at full length from August 1893 onwards into the next year; it was begun as a serial story in *Harper's Magazine,* in November 1896; it was published in 1896. Hardy says of it : " For a novel addressed by a man to men and women of full age; which attempts to deal unaffectedly with the fret and fever, derision and disaster, that may press in the wake of the strongest passion known to humanity, and to point, without a mincing of words, the tragedy of unfulfilled aims. I am not aware that there is anything in the handling to which exception can be taken. Like former productions of this pen, *Jude the Obscure* is simply an endeavour to give shape and coherence to a series of seeming or personal impressions, the question of their consistency or their discordances, of their permanence or their transitoriness, being regarded as not of the first moment." That certainly is a noble defence, and it is written nobly. Only, can one take for granted that an Author knows inevitably the conception and the execution of his

Work or of his Travail? That is doubt-ful.

Hardy says of *The Woodlanders* : " In the present novel, as in one or two others of this series which involve the question of matrimonial divergence, the immortal puzzle—given the Man and Woman, how to find a basis for their sexual relation—is left where it stood; and it is tacitly assumed for the purpose of the story that no doubt of the depravity of the erratic heart who feels some third person to be better suited to him or her rather than the one with whom he has contracted to live, enters the head of reader or writer for a moment. From the point of view of marriage as a distinct contract or under-taking, decided on by two people fully cognizant of all its possible issues, and competent to carry them through, this assumption is, of course, logical." The immortal puzzle : that is the basis of all great novels. Balzac discovered for himself, and for others after him, a method of unemotional, minute, slightly ironical analysis, which has fascinated modern minds, partly because it has seemed to dispense with those difficulties of creation, of creation in the block, which the triumphs of Balzac have only accentuated. Gorot, Valérie Marneffe, Père Goriot, Madame de Mortsauf even, are called up before us after the same manner as Othello or Don Quixote; their actions express them so significantly that they seem to be independent of their creator : Balzac stakes all upon each creation, and leaves us no choice but to accept or reject each as a whole, exactly as we should a human being.

In the novels of Hardy there is an
immense amount of sardonic humour
which can at times become diabolical;
there is also an immense amount of
tragedy and a certain amount of pathos.
When I think of Daudet who had
southern blood in his veins, one finds that,
caring, as he thought, supremely for life,
he cared really for that surprising, bewildering pantomime which life seems to be
to those who watch its coloured movement, its flickering lights, its changing
costumes, its powdered faces, without
looking through the eyes into the hearts
of the dancers. To the great artist life is
indeed a comedy, but it is a comedy on
which his own part is to stand silently in

the wings, occasionally ringing down the curtain. Once his characters are in motion —having endowed them with what he has felt in his heart and in his imagination— he surveys them with the controlling indifference of Fate. Dolobelle, the actor in *Fromon Jeune,* the Nabob, the Kings in exile, are studies of " humours " in Ben Jonson's sense; they are not studies of character. Pathos such as Daudet's comes from the man to whom life is an entertainment absolutely entertaining; he dreads only its ending, or an accident which may interrupt it. It is from the South that he has taken those honeyed and delicate short stories which, to those who know Provence as I do and can read Provençal, have the very taste of the soil.

He is a quick observer, but never a disinterested observer, for he is a sentimentalist among realists. All his power comes from the immediateness of his appeal to the heart : to the intellect he never appeals. He appeals, certainly, to the average human sympathies, and he appeals to them with his power of writing a story which shall absorb the interest as an English novel absorbs the interest, by its comedy, using that word in its broadest sense. Even *Sapho* is essentially comedy, and Daudet is not far from being at his best in that brief, emphatic tale of a dull and disenchanted Bohemia. Others before Daudet had studied the life of a woman professionally " gay." Huysmans had studied it brutally, with a deliberate lack of sympathy, in *Marthe*. Zola had studied it, with his exuberant method of representing, not the living woman, but the pattern of her trade. Goncourt had studied it, delicately, but with a subtlety which digresses into merely humanitarian

considerations in *La Fille Elisa*. Daudet
gives us neither vice nor romance, but the
average painted dreariness of *le collage*.
Yet he is not content with painting his
picture : he must moralise, arrange with
an appeal to the sympathies as definitely
sentimental, for all its disguises, as that
of *La Dame aux Camélias*. He cannot
be as indifferently just to his Sapho as
Flaubert in *L'Education Sentimentale*
is indifferently and supremely just to
Rosanette. And partly for this very
reason, it is only the external semblance
of life which he gives; rarely the heart,
never the soul. In his vivid, passionate,
tragically pathetic studies of "that exciting
Paris " (it is his own word), " where the
dolls talk " Daudet is entertaining as a
fairy tale.

In the *New Review,* 1890, Hardy con-
tributed an article on *Candour in Fiction* :

"Our imagination is the slave of stolid circumstance; and the noonday flow of circumstance which finds expression of the literature of Fiction is no exception to the general law. We would suggest that the most natural way of presenting them, the method most in accordance with the view themselves, seems to be by a procedure mainly impassive in its tone and tragic in its developments. Things move in cycles, one requires original treatment: treatment which shows Nature's universal will not of essential laws, but of those laws framed merely as social expedients by humanity, without a basis in the heart of things. In the representation of the world the passions ought to be proportioned as in the world itself. This was the interest which was excited in the minds of the Athenians by their immortal tragedies. Life being a physiological fact, its honest portrayal must be largely conceived with for one thing, the relation of the Sexes, and of the substitution of certain catastrophies for those based upon sexual relationship as it is. To this expansion society imposes a well nigh insuperable bar. The magazine does not foster the growth of the novel which reflects and reveals life. A comprehensive sequence of the ruling passion, however moral in its ultimate bearing, must not be put on paper as the foundation of imaginative work. The rush of broken commandments is as necessary an accompaniment to the catastrophe of a tragedy as the noise of drum and cymbals to a triumphal march. In a ramification of the profounder passions, the treatment of which makes the great style, something "unsuitable" is sure to arise. When a great story is printed month by month in a magazine

before the remainder is written, the author
asks himself, what will his characters do
next? What would probably happen to
them, given such beginnings? On his life
and conscience, though he had not fore-
seen the thing, only one event could
possibly happen, and that therefore he
should narrate, as he calls himself a
faithful artist. Were the objections of the
scrupulous limited to a prurient treatment of the relations of the sexes, or to any
view of vice calculated to undermine the
essential principles of social order, all
honest lovers of literature would be in
accord with them. But the writer may
print the *not* of his broken command-
ment in letters of flame; it makes no
difference. A question which should be
wholly a question of treatment is con-
fusedly regarded as a question of subject."

In 1871 Hardy gave his opinion on the

Science of Fiction : " Nothing but the illusion of truth can permanently please, and when the old illusions begin to be penetrated, a more natural magic has to be supplied. Creativeness in its full and ancient sense—the making a thing or situation out of nothing that ever was before—is apparently ceasing to satisfy a world which no longer believes in the Abnormal.

" Once in a crowd a listener heard a needy and illiterate woman say of another poor and haggard woman who had lost her little son years before : ' You can see the ghost of that child in her face even now.' That speaker was one, who though she could probably neither read nor write, had the true means toward the Science of Fiction innate within her : a power of observation informed by a living heart."
How absolutely that applies to Hardy

as the man and the novelist combined.
This reminds me of some lines of Landor,
that bite as well as shine; those of the
drunken woman who has drowned her
child.

Febe.   I sometimes wish 'twere back
           again.

Frederic. To cry?

Febe.   Eh! It *does* cry ere the first
           sea-mew cries;
           It wakes me many mornings,
           many nights,
           And fields of poppies cannot
           quiet it.

One Saturday when I walked along the
Edgware Road, between two opposing
currents of evil smells, I heard a man who
was lurching on the pavement say in
a contemptuous comment: "Twelve
o'clock! We may all be dead by twelve
o'clock!" He seemed to me to sum up the
philosophy of that crowd, its littleness,

its hard unconcern, its failure to be interested. Nothing matters, he seemed to say for them; let us drag out our time until the time is over, and the sooner it is over the better.

Apart from Balzac's women, and some
of the women one finds in the novels of
Meredith and Tolstoi, Eustacia Vye is
one of the greatest achievements in modern fiction : she is one whose imagination is complex, whose beauty is subtle
and passionate and sombre and enigma-
tical and, above all, intensely fascinating;
she is an extraordinary mixture of good
and evil; morbid, brooding, strangely
sensitive and magnetically nervous :
a mass of contradictions, for she cannot
fathom the mystery of her being : she
is immensely proud of her southern
beauty; she is a creature whose impulse
and instinct war with one another : she

is as essentially lonely as that tremendous
loneliness of Egdon Heath, which, when
I have traversed it, seemed to me endless,
bewildering, mysterious, menacing, lux-
urious, reptilian, with cruel-looking roads
that intersect one another, creep down
some steep and vanish out of one's
vision into some deeper steep; which
when night comes on and a sombre darkness begins to envelop it, crawling
onward and inward like a legion of
coiling and clinging serpents, one imagines, I did at least, the sudden rush of
assassins who stab you in the back, and
of cut-throats who leave you dead in some
deep ditch : and all these thin lines that
intersect the Heath turn more and more
sinister, as one of them seems to plunge
headlong just beyond you into some
unseen abyss. And there must be something in it, which, to Hardy who has

explored every inch of it, attains sublimity.

Egdon Heath, which I have so often wandered over, seemed to me at night something God might have cursed, for its breath is that of death in life, and its invisible tenacity is that of an Incubus. It lives and writhes : just as a legion of serpents as I have said, writhe and live : and there are grim and ghastly spots in it which made my blood curdle, and which seemed to imbibe poison. There are deadly hollows and evil thickets. I thought of *Childe Roland to the Dark Tower came* : this journey across a strange and dreadful country is one of the ghastliest and most vivid in all poetry : ghastly without hope, without alleviation : the poet's imagination flashes like lightning cleaving the darkness of midnight, and illuminating point by point the horrors of the landscape.

A sudden little river crossed my path
As unexpected as the serpent comes.
No sluggish tide congenial to the gloom's—
This, as it frothed by, might have been a bath
For the fiend's glowing hoof—to see the wrath
Of its black eddy bespate with flacks and spumes.

"The place," wrote Hardy, "became full of a watchful intentness now. When other things sank brooding to sleep, the Heath appeared slowly to awaken and listen. Every night its Titanic form seemed to await something; but it had waited thus, unmoved, during so many centuries through the Crises of so many things, that it could only be imagined to await one last Crisis—the final overthrow."

"Eustasia," writes Hardy, "was in person full limbed and somewhat heavy; without ruddiness, as without pallor; and soft to the touch as a cloud. To see her hair was to fancy that a whole winter did not contain darkness enough to form its shadow. Her nerves extended into those tresses, and her temper could always be softened by stroking them down. When her hair was brushed she would insensibly sink into stillness and look like the Sphinx. She had Pagan eyes, full of nocturnal mysteries. Assuming that the souls of men and women were visible essences, you could fancy the colour of Eustasia's soul to be flame-like. The mouth seemed formed less to speak than to quiver, less to quiver than to kiss. Her appearance accorded well with the smouldering rebelliousness, as of Hades, and the strange splendour of her beauty was the real surface of the sad and stifled warmth within her. To be loved to madness—such was her great desire. She thought of Destiny with an ever-growing conscious-ness of cruelty, which tended to brand actions of reckless unconventionality, framed to snatch a year's, a week's, even an hour's passion from anywhere where it could be won. Through want of it she had sung without being merry, possessed without enjoying, achieved without triumphing. In regard to love she knew by prevision what most women learn only by experience. She could utter oracles of Delphian ambiguity when she did not choose to be direct. In heaven she will probably sit between the Helöises and the Cleopatras."

Does not this show in Hardy a fearful and wonderful knowledge of the hearts of women, women I mean in their youth and splendour and tragic passion, which one rarely finds in fiction, outside Balzac and Meredith and at times in Tolstoi?

> You have not known
> The dreadful heart of woman, who one day
> Forgets the old and takes the new to heart,
> Forgets what man remembers, and therewith
> Forgets the man.

Yet all these wonderful women, from Lilith onward, including Helen of Troy, Cleopatra, Faustina, Messalina, Valerie Marneffe and Rhoda Fleming, are said to have forgotten the man. And yet did they? I doubt it. For every woman remembers to the end of her days the one passionate Lover who constrained her to be his mistress. And yet to quote Rossetti again :

> Look that you turn not now—she's at your back !
> Gather your robe up, Father, and sit close,
> Or she'll sit down on it and send you mad.
>   If you mistake my words
> And so absolve me, Father, the great sin
> Is yours, not mine : mark this : your soul shall burn
> With mine for it. I have seen pictures where
> Souls burned with Latin shriekings in their mouths :
> Shall my end be as theirs? Nay, but I know
> 'Tis you shall shriek in Latin. Some bell rings,
> Rings through my brain : it strikes the hour in hell.

Hardy is a fatalist and he studies the

workings of fate in the chief living and disturbing influence in life, women. His view of woman is much more French than English (he has French blood in him as well as Dorset blood); it is subtle, curiously cruel, not as tolerant as it seems, mostly a man's point of view, and not, as with Meredith, men's and women's at one. No one has created more attractive women whom a man would have been more likely to love, or more likely to regret loving. He sees all that in woman is alluring and her versatility, all that is unreliable in her will and mind, and what in her is essentially irresponsible for good and evil. At the same time, there is almost no passion in his work, neither the creator nor any of his characters ever seeming able to pass beyond the state of curiosity under the influence of any emotion.

No one has ever studied so scrupulously
as Hardy the effect of emotion on inanimate things, or has seen emotion so vividly
in people. For instance : " Terror was
upon her white face as she saw it, her
cheek was flaccid, and her mouth had
almost the aspect of a round little hole."
The reference to the mouth reminds me
of some verses I wrote in Paris.

Eyelids of women, little curls of hair,
A little nose curved softly, like a shell,
A red mouth like a wound, a mocking veil :
Phantoms, before the dawn, how phantom-fair !
And every woman with beseeching eyes,
Or with enticing eyes, or amorous,
Offers herself, a rose, and craves of us
A rose's place among our memories.

But so intense is Hardy's preoccupation
with these visual appeals that he sometimes cannot resist noting a minute
appearance though in the very moment
of assuring us that the person looking on
did not see it. And it is this power of

seeing to excess and being limited to sight which is often strange revealing, that leaves him, at times, helpless before the naked words that a situation supremely seen demands for its completion. The one failing in what is perhaps his master-piece, *The Return of the Native*, is in the words put into the mouth of Eustasia and Yeobright in the perfectly imagined scene before the mirror, a scene which should be the culminating scene in the book; and it is, all but the words: the words are crackle and tinsel. And yet how tragic are those sentences, " He came behind her and she saw his face in the glass. It was ashy, haggard, and terrible. Instead of starting towards him in sorrowful surprise, as even Eustasia's, undemonstrative wife as she was, would have done in days before she burdened herself with a secret, she remained motionless, looking at him

in the gloom.   And while she looked
the carmine flush with which warmth and
sound sleep had suffused her cheeks and
neck dissolved from view, and the death-
like pallor in his face flew across to hers."

Facts, one knows, are done with:
stories of mere action gallop across the
brain and are gone; but in Hardy there
is a vision and interpretation, a vivid
sense of life as a growth out of the earth,
and as much a mystery between soil and
sky as the corn is, which will draw men
back to the stories with an interest which
outlasts their interest in the story.   Too
often in his books there is too much story,
which makes their plots extend into almost
inextricable entanglements.   Is it I wonder
on account of that concealed poetry, never
absent, though often unseen, which gives
to these fantastic or real histories a
meaning beyond the meaning of the facts,

around it like an atmosphere? What seems puzzling and bewildering is that Hardy, who is above all a story-teller and whose stories are of a kind that rouse suspense and satisfy it, can be read more than once, and never be quite without novelty. Morris was an incomparable story-teller; or, to be exact, he can be compared in the literal sense only with Chaucer: and it would be rash to say, without premeditation, that Chaucer was a better story-teller than Morris. Chaucer had an incomparably wider range of mastery; he had to his hand the " humours " of all the world. Morris has none of Chaucer's sturdy humanity, his dramatic power, his directness; above all, none of his humour. It was because Morris felt himself so painfully an artist that he first set himself to be one with others if he could : he was always ready to help them

as egoists usually are, but without love.
Yes, Morris was lacking in that one
quintessential quality : Love.

I have often wondered why there are
so few novels which can be read twice;
while all good poetry can be read over
and over. Is it something inherent in the
form, one of the reasons in nature why a
novel cannot be of the same supreme
imaginative substance as a poem? I think
it is, and that it will never be otherwise.
Certain novels literally seem to cry from
their shelves with almost the insistence
of a lyric, while for the most part a story
read is a story done with. I can always
re-read *Lavengro.* Balzac is always good
to re-read, but not Tolstoi : and I couple
two of the giants.

What is it makes up the main value
and fascination of Hardy, and how is it
that what at first seems and are defects,

bits of formal preaching, uncouthness, grotesque ironies of idea and event, come at the end to seem either good in themselves or good where they are, a part of the man if not of the artist? The story has an astonishing interest and one begins to read it for the story: that of a story-teller whose plots are mostly more than plausible. Next after the story-teller one comes on the philosopher, who is at once sinister and dejected, and who might check your attention to his narrative if you were too attentive to his criticism of it. Then a new meaning comes into the facts as you notice his curious attitude in regard to these facts, and you may be content to stop and be fed with thoughts by the philosopher. At the very last, if not at the very beginning, you will find the poet, and you need look for nothing beyond. I am inclined to question if any novelist has been more truly a poet without ceasing to be in the true sense a novelist. The poetry of his novels is a poetry of roots, and it is a voice of the earth.

In his verse, there is something brooding, obscure, tremulous, half inarticulate, as he meditates over men, nature and destiny: nature, "waking by sounds alone" and Fate, who sees and feels. In one strange, dreary, ironical song of science, Nature laments that her best achievement, Man, has become disenchanted with her in his ungrateful discontent with himself. Blind and dumb forces conjecture, speak, half awakening out of sleep, turning back heavily to sleep again. Here is a poet who is sorry for Nature, who feels the earth and the roots, as if he has sap in his veins instead of blood, and could get closer than any other man to the things of the Earth.

"Heine," wrote Swinburne, "that snake of the Hebrew Paradise—'a smooth-lipped serpent, surely high inspired'—was never inspired more truly by the serpent's genius of virulent wisdom than when he uttered, in a most characteristic hiss of sarcasm, a sentence as conclusive in its judgment as venomous in its malignity, describing Musset before he had reached middle age as 'a young man with a very fine career—behind him' (*un jeune homme d'un bien beau passé*)." He adds: "At a too early date in the career of Musset it must have been evident to others besides his amiable Hebrew admirer that his Muse at all events 'n'avait plus rien dans le ventre' and was most undeniably 'maigre à faire peur—ou plutôt à faire pitié.'" There is a curious similarity between the light and sarcastic, half-tragic and half-pathetic,

songs of Heine in certain of Hardy's
most effective short poems, such as *The
Fiddler.*

> The fiddler knows what's brewing
> To the lilt of his lyric wiles :
> The fiddler knows what rueing
> Will come of this night's smiles !
>
> He sees couples join them for dancing,
> And afterwards joining for life,
> He sees them pay high for their prancing
> By a welter of wedded strife.
>
> He twangs : " Music hails from the devil,
> Though vaunted to come from heaven,
> For it makes people do at a revel
> What multiplies sins by seven.
>
> There's many a heart now mangled
> And waiting its time to go,
> Whose tendrils were first entangled
> By my sweet viol and bow !"

The origin of these lines is Heine's;
but Hardy never comes near the ghastly
splendour of these two stanzas of Heine's :

> The Mother flings her Bible
> With rage in his famished face.
> " Accursed of God ! with these footpads
> The gallows wouldst thou grace ? "

They hear a tap at the window,
　　There comes a beckoning hand :
Without, in his worn black cassock,
　　They see the dead Father stand.

Among Hardy's *Satires of Circumstance* one strikes me as being immensely cynical, written in a metre used by Browning, but much more weird than anything Browning wrote.

IN THE NUPTIAL CHAMBER.

"O that mastering tune!" And up on the bed
Like a lace-robed phantom springs the bride;
"And why?" asks the man she had that day wed,
With a start, as the band plays on outside.
"It's the townsfolk's cheery compliment
Because of our marriage, my Innocent."

"O but you don't know! 'Tis the passionate air
To which my old Love waltzed with me,
And I swore as we spun that none should share
My home, my kisses, till death, save he!
And he dominates me and thrills me through,
And it's he I embrace while embracing you!"

The origin of this poem, I imagine, is due to Hardy's immense admiration of the genius of John Donne, whose senses speak with unparalleled directness, as in those elegies which must remain the model in English of masculine sensual sobriety. In a series of hate poems, of which I will quote the finest, he gives expression to a whole region of profound human sentiment which has never been expressed out of Catullus, with such intolerable truth.

When by thy scorn, O murderess, I am dead,
And that thou think'st thee free
From all solicitation from me,
Then shall my ghost come to thy bed,
And thee, feigned vestal, in worse arms shall see :
Then thy sick taper will begin to wink,
And he, whose thou art then, being tired before,
Will, if thou stir, or pinch to wake him, think
Thou call'st for more,
And, in false sleep, will from thee shrink;
And then, poor aspen wretch, neglected thou
Bathed in cold quicksilver sweat, will lie
A verier ghost than I.
What I will say, I will not tell thee now,
Let that preserve thee; and since my love is spent,
I'd rather thou should'st painfully repent,
Than by my threatenings rest still innocent.

There is no question of comparing Hardy as a Ballad writer with the writer of such an immortal ballad as a *Lyke Wake Dirge*.

This ae nighte, this ae nighte,
—*Every nighte and alle,*
Fire and sleet, and candle-lighte,
And Christe receive thy saule.

If meat or drinke thou ne'er gav'st nane,
—*Every nighte and alle,*
The fire will burn thee to the bare bane;
And Christe receive thy saule.

Nor can I compare his few ballads with these that are incomparable: *The Ancient Mariner, Sister Helen, Rose Mary* and Meredith's *Margaret's Bridal Eve*. In the first one, a new supernaturalism comes into poetry: the impossible, frankly accepted on its own terms: the creation of a new atmosphere, outside the known world, which becomes as real as the air about us, and yet never loses its strangeness : it presents to us the utmost physical and spiritual horror, not only without disgust, but with an alluring beauty. *Sister Helen* is an arduous sensuous tragedy, where the soul and the senses of this creature endure "the terrible Love turned to Hate, perhaps the deadliest of all passion-woven complexities," visualised by pure magic, on a small space of the earth that lies between Hell and Heaven : and she turned witch for a reason, transformed into a breathing and destroying angel of no perdition, is driven by an absolute sense of vengeance to destroy her lover's life. In *Rose Mary* Rossetti seems to me, in the tragic woof of this conception in which there are traces of wizardry, to have reclothed himself in the enchanter's robes of Coleridge. The ballad of Meredith is at once pathetic and tragic and ominous.

A Sunday Morning Tragedy of Hardy has the beat of the old ballad, which adds weighty emphasis to every stanza : it has, on the whole, that quintessence of tragic narrative and construction in which I recognise the ballad form, but not an entire mastery of that form. *A Tramp-Woman's Tragedy* is intensely dramatic : essentially it might have been turned into a One Act Prose Play. The metre is original, so is the rhythm, and the beat of the stanzas. Hardy gets that heavy emphasis by the repetition in every stanza, thus :

> From Wynward's Gap the live-long day,
>   The live-long day,
> We beat afoot the northward way,
>   We had travelled times before.
> The sun-blaze burning on our backs,
> Our shoulders sticking to our packs,
> By fosseway, fields, and turnpike tracks
>   We skirted sad Sedge Moor.

The crisis occurs in the taproom of a

tavern, when the woman makes obvious love to her fancy-man in mere wantonness.

> Inside the settle all a-row—
>   All four a-row,
> We sat, I next to John, to show
>   That he had wooed and won.
> And then he took me on his knee,
> And swore it was his turn to be
> My favoured mate, and Mother Lee
>   Passed to my former one.

She is with child and her fancy-man asks her whose child it is. She nods her head : he springs up and stabs John.

> Thereaft I walked the world alone,
>   Alone, alone !
> On his death-day I gave my groan
>   And dropt his dead-born child.
> 'Twas nigh the jail, beneath a tree,
> None tending me; for Mother Lee
> Had died at Glaston, leaving me
>   Unfriended on the wild.

Writing on Campbell's *Battle of the Baltic,* I said that such things are unique in English. The structure, with its long line moving slowly to the pause, at which the three heavily weighted, yet, as it were, proudly prancing syllables fall over and are matched by the three syllables which make the last line, the whole rhythmical scheme, unlike anything that has been done before, has left its mark upon whatever in that line has been done finely since : upon Browning in *Hervé Riel,* and upon Tennyson in *The Revenge.*

> Of Nelson and the North
> Sing the glorious day's renown,
> When to battle fierce came forth
> All the might of Denmark's crown,
> And her arms along the deep proudly shone;
> By each gun the lighted brand
> In a bold determined hand,
> And the Prince of all the land
> Led them on.

Who else but Hardy could have written this crabbed, subtle, strangely impressive poem, *An August Night?*

> A shaded lamp and a waving blind,
> And the beat of a clock from a distant floor :
> On this scene enter—winged, horned and spined——
> A longlegs, a moth and a dumbledore;
> While 'mid my page there idly stands
> A sleepy fly, that rubs its hands.

There meet we five, in this still place,
At this point of time, at this point in space.
—My guests parade my new-penned ink,
Or bang at the lamp-glass, whirl, and sink.
"God's humblest, they!" I muse. Yet why?
They know Earth-secrets that know not I.

Now compare these lines with *Adam,
Lilith and Eve.*

One day it thundered and lightened.
Two women, fairly frightened,
Sank to their knees, transformed, transfixed,
At the feet of the man who sat betwixt;
And " Mercy!" cried each, "If I tell the truth
Of a passage in my youth!"

Said This : " Do you mind the morning
I met your soul with scorning?"
As the worst of the venom left my lips,
I thought, " If, despite this lie, he strips
The mask from my soul with a kiss—I crawl,
His slave—soul, body and all!"

Said That : " We stood to be married;
The priest, or someone, tarried;
' If Paradise-door prove locked?' smiled you,
I thought, as I nodded, smiling too,
' Did one, that's away, arrive—too late
Nor soon should unlock Hell's gate!' "

It ceased to lighten and thunder.
Up started both in wonder,
Looked round, and saw that the day was clear,
. Then laughed, " Confess, you believe us. Dear !"
" I saw through the joke !" the man replied
They seated themselves beside.

Was anything more poignant and
suggestive, more primitive and ironical,
more subtle and more sinister, ever
written? Browning rarely excelled it in
his most wonderful style of penetrating
bitter-sweetness and exquisitely tempered
intensity. And it is essentially dramatic.
It is thrilling, and alive with that satirical
power which seems to be latent in such
poems, 'darting out with a vivid and
convincing shock from time to time. The
two women in question have been guilty
of two separate forms of sinning; both
have signally failed in fulfilling their
Destinies. Both, on the sudden, struck by
a sinister crisis, have confessed what they